CW01637832

Living the dream of God

A guided prayer journal on 40 key insights from Scripture, Christian Catholic tradition and practical spirituality

Dominic Michael Sultana

Living the dream of God

Copyright © 2022 Dominic Michael Sultana
All rights reserved,
including the right of reproduction
in whole or in part in any form.

For information regarding special discounts for bulk purchases,
please get in touch with Fr Dominic at to.fr.dominic@gmail.com

God Mediation Publications
Practical Spiritual Growth Series Vol. I
21, Racecourse Street, Xaghra, Gozo
XRA2010, Malta EU
https://www.godmediation.world

in association with
Teresian Media Publications
Carmelite Priory, Boars Hill, Oxford
OX1 5HB, United Kingdom

Nihil obstat, datum die 8 octobris 2022,
Mons. Laurentius Sciberras, Cens. Theol.

Imprimatur Gaudisii, die 12 octobris 2022,
Mons. Tarcisius Camilleri, Vic. Gen.

ISBN 978-9918-9554-0-4

To all those seeking

the will of God

Preface

Christians can easily get discouraged and disheartened in today's world, hit by the COVID-19 pandemic, war conflicts, economic crises, uncertainties, and lack of faith.

Fr. Dominic Sultana, in Living the dream of God, offers excellent aid to help those of us who may at times feel on the verge of a breakdown and even sorely tempted to abandon the journey of faith, the Church, and even God.

Countless books about love and faith exist, but very few are about hope. It is so vital for every Christian to be encouraged to grow in trust and strengthen his faith through a divine hope well-grounded in the dream God has for each person.

"Pilgrims of Hope" is the motto chosen by Pope Francis for the Jubilee year 2025. Reading and meditating Living the dream of God could be the best personal preparation for this significant Church celebration.

This book is like a loyal companion that caters to the reader's current needs and can guide them to become more human and holy. While reading this book, one can discover that 'No one should lose heart!' The Spirit will aid all who will risk once more and give him the slightest chance.

LIVING THE DREAM OF GOD is an accurate guide to those searching for authentic meaning in life. With the strength given by the Holy Spirit, the giver of life, one discovers meaning in life and a reason to move forward.

LIVING THE DREAM OF GOD is a handy tool for Christian formators, Spiritual Directors and those who lead spiritual exercises for the clergy and lay people.

Based mainly on Holy Scriptures, LIVING THE DREAM OF GOD is a book to read and read again. It is more like a workbook, leading to spiritual exercises and prayer. Inspired by St. Ignatius of Loyola, Saint John of the Cross and Theresa of Avila, the exercises found in this book can easily promote the experience of the Spirit who dwells in each one of us.

✠ **Anthony Teuma**
Bishop of Gozo Diocese, Malta

CONTENTS

Why have you picked this book?

Why have you picked this book, Living the Dream of God?

Is it because you lack an aim in life? Is it because you are a curious explorer? Is it because someone else suggested this book to you? Or is it something else entirely?

Whatever the reason might have been, in this book, you can find answers to most questions.

You might be saying that this is a bold statement. However, before allowing your mind to judge the content of this book, I would like to share something with you.

Have you ever thought that – while you might not be happy about your actual situation – **the fact that you are alive means there is still an opportunity for you to turn things around and dream again?**

Someone once said that **'the measure of a person's will is determined by what a person is willing to dream over losing.'**

Thus, I invite you to ask yourself: Are you ready to dream again at this point in your life? Do you consider it too late or too early to dream? Are you willing to lose some of your securities to give birth to your most heartfelt and genuine dreams?

The Crossroad

Such questions put you at a crossroads. And when someone is at a crossroads, usually, one faces the winner and quitter in oneself.

Thus **you have a choice to make. You can either listen to the winner or the quitter inside you.**

If you are a quitter, please stop wasting your time reading this book. Make it available for others willing more than you to "fight the good fight of the faith" (1 Timothy 6:12). You can donate it to someone or sell it online.

If you decide not to quit, this book intends to help you listen to the winner inside you, as the quitter will never take you to the road your God wants you to travel.

Please state why you did not quit reading.

____

____

____

Choosing the Dream

What could be some of the dreams you are following?

Maybe it is a dream related to your physical or mental health, such as losing weight, breaking an addiction, or finding yourself after a trauma or during an illness.

Perhaps it is a dream related to your family, like, for example, finding a life partner, seeing your family restored, reconnecting with your children, or maybe learning to live on your own after your partner died or left you.

Or perhaps, it might be a dream related to your Church, like starting a new mission or a new group. The list could be endless. These are only some ideas.

More probably, however, you already know your dreams, at least in a vague and opaque way.

Take your time now to acknowledge some of your dreams and desires in writing.

If your dreams are unclear or dormant at this point in your life, this book might help you revive them. **Just be aware that there is still time to dream because you are alive.** Remember that you can always dream even if you are on the brink of death.

Facing the pain

But sometimes, as life goes on, day after day, month after month, even year after year, we don't see anything changing. In moments like this, it's easy to get discouraged and think: 'This will never happen...' 'This is as good as it gets. I have to learn to live with it...'.

Pain is a part of life. We all go through losses, setbacks, and disappointments. In such moments it's easy to get disheartened and sometimes even bitter. You can start moaning continuously: 'Why is this happening to me?' Such a statement can lead to increased negative feelings like anger, guilt, fear and anxiety.

The issue is always what you do in times of pain. **Even though no one likes pain, it can lead you to new alternatives, possibilities and choices that can help you see the world from a different perspective.**

Eventually, the pain will ease. Sometimes it passes away entirely. Other times you manage to tolerate it, learn how to live with it, or give it a sublime meaning. Whatever happens, you will be different after such a period of pain.

During such challenging times, when you are in pain, uncomfortable, or dealing with a failure, frustration, illness or loss, you can easily let it overwhelm you. You can come out of such challenging times feeling bitter, or you can become better and stronger. **How the pain changes you is up to you!**

You can come out defeated by giving up on your dreams. Or you can acquire a new passion, new fire, and be excited about the new opportunities ahead of you.

Through such painful periods, you can become a whiner, or you can become a warrior.

Take some time now to acknowledge in writing what might be some of your typical reactions to pain, frustrations, anger, guilt, fear and anxiety.

THE ATTITUDE OF A WINNER

For those aiming to live God's dream, there is no room for becoming bitter or defeated. There is no room for whining. Jesus was clear: "If any want to become my followers, let them deny themselves and take up their cross daily and follow me" (Luke 9:23).

Scripture continually reminds us that **we must be warriors living God's dream**. Saint Paul urges us to "fight the good fight of the faith" (1 Timothy 6:12) and to "train yourself in godliness" (1 Timothy 4:7) to "let the same mind be in you that was in Christ Jesus" (Philippians 2:5).

The victory in this war is made possible with the aid of the Holy Spirit since "no one can say 'Jesus is Lord' except by the Holy Spirit" (1 Corinthians 12:3; cf. Romans 8:9).

Scripture also reminds us that "Christ also suffered for you, leaving you an example, so that you should follow in his steps" (1 Peter 2:21). It also reminds us that "The stone that the builders rejected, has become the chief cornerstone" (Psalm 118:22).

Everything that we might think was useless, harmful, or without any sense, in the end, may turn out to be the cornerstone of our lives.

What may be some of your impressions regarding this statement?

CHRIST, THE WINNER'S MODEL

Just envision the life of Christ, and observe how he ended up crucified by the same people who had benefitted from his teachings and miracles.

> He "who, though he was in the form of God, did not regard equality with God as something to be exploited, but emptied himself, taking the form of a slave, being born in human likeness. And being found in human form, he humbled himself and became obedient to the point of death—even death on a cross."

But the story did not stop there because, as Saint Paul continues to explain:

> "Therefore God also highly exalted him and gave him the name that is above every name, so that at the name of Jesus every knee should bend, in heaven and on earth and under the earth, and every tongue should confess that Jesus Christ is Lord, to the glory of God the Father" (Philippians 2: 6-11).

We realize that we cannot reflect God's goodness like Christ did. But our commitment to Christ under the guidance of the Holy Spirit (1 Corinthians 6:19) enables us to grow into God's likeness.

The Holy Spirit continually pulls us back from our sins and failures to live God's dream since "God has sent the Spirit of his Son into our hearts, crying, 'Abba! Father!'" (Galatians 4:6).

God's dream for you: Being in union with him for eternity

God's dream in us continues to unfold during our entire earthly journey.

It's a process that happens within the context of a life journey of unions and ruptures, leading to the eternal union with God in Christ.

A journey that endures until one day, heaven and earth will become one and God's dream to dwell among his people in peace and unity will be realized.

We should look forward to the actualization of this dream because Christ assured a place for us in heaven:

> "Do not let your heart be troubled. [...] In my Father's house there are many dwelling places" (John 14:1-2).

A PREVIEW OF ETERNITY

We must always keep this ultimate heavenly aim in front of our eyes. Thus, inspired by the words of St. Stephen at the moment of his death, I invite you now to experience "What no eye has seen, nor ear heard, nor the human heart conceived, what God has prepared for those who love him" (1 Corinthians 2:9). "Look", St. Stephen said, "I see the heavens opened and the Son of Man standing at the right hand of God!" (Acts 7:55-56).

Thus for a moment, through the eyes of faith and imagination, you can now start imagining this scene of yourself in front of God in heaven. Take all the time you need, and maybe while closing your eyes, envision this scene clearer, bigger, and three-dimensional.

Add also to this scene the sound of the voice of the angels singing, "Holy, holy, holy, the Lord God the Almighty, who was and is to come" (Revelations 4:8).

And while you are hearing this eternal song, inhale the smell of incense, and notice "the twenty-four elders [..] each holding a harp and golden bowls full of incense, which are the prayers of the saints" (Revelations 5:8).

And now, while taking a deep breath, imagine yourself in front of God. And while you are still hearing the eternal song with your nostrils filled with the fragrance of incense, figure yourself in a state of eternity, where time matters no more and where you are free of your body, and enter a state of thanksgiving.

And while you are in this state, listen to Jesus telling you:

> "Come, you that are blessed by my Father, inherit the kingdom prepared for you from the foundation of the world; for I was hungry and you gave me food, I was thirsty and you gave me something to drink, I was a stranger and you welcomed me, I was naked and you gave me clothing, I was sick and you took care of me, I was in prison and you visited me".

And imagine yourself saying,

> "Lord, when was it that we saw you hungry and gave you food, or thirsty and gave you something to drink? And when was it that we saw you a stranger and welcomed you, or naked

> and gave you clothing? And when was it that we saw you sick or in prison and visited you?"

And Jesus will tell you,

> "Truly I tell you, just as you did it to one of the least of these who are members of my family, you did it to me" (Matthew 25:34-40).

And while you hear this, turn back and look at your life at the present moment, and imagine yourself at home, at work, in your community, and notice that in every situation, you are acting in love because now you know that "Heaven and earth will pass away," (Luke 21,33). Still, the word of God does not pass away.

Loving God and others is the easiest thing for you because the law of love is imprinted in your heart (Romans 2:14-16).

You are created in God's image (Genesis 1:26), and since God is love, **your heart will not find rest if not immersed in love towards God and others**.

And if you ever doubt what your heart is telling you, look at Christ. You can meet your own incarnated heart through his words and deeds, since through Christ, what is written in your heart was made flesh (John 1:14). After all, you are his image.

More than this, like Christ, **you are God's beloved child** (Ephesians 1:4-5), and **Christ is your brother** (Matthew 12:50; 28:10; John 20:17).

What may be some of your impressions on what awaits you in heaven? How may you orientate your life more towards this ultimate aim?

UNION WITH GOD HERE ON EARTH

This union with God that awaits us in heaven could also be lived here and now on earth. It is a gift that we must accept.

This is because the Holy Spirit does not substitute our freedom to 'accept' or 'deny' this gift; however, it 'generates' and 'sustains' it. To do so, we need to strive to free ourselves from what is evil so as to be free to glorify God.

All this can happen for us through **a process of discernment**. A process that helps us

> "not [to] be conformed to this world, but be transformed by the renewing of your minds, so that you may discern what is the will of God–what is good and acceptable and perfect" (Romans 12:2).

An effort to "be conformed to the image of his Son" (Romans 8:29), our Lord Jesus Christ.

The opportunity to live God's Dream

If you look at the world around you, your family, your place of work, and places where you entertain yourself, you can notice that **this world is filled with opportunities for you to be happy by striving to find and live God's dream for you**. It is filled with opportunities to gain the inner freedom to reach what you are destined for.

Stop thinking about regrets. Regret that you have not done this thing or the other. **Maybe it was not God's time for you then**. Now you have gained more experience.

And while acknowledging that physically you are getting older, remember that in twenty years' time, if you do not react now, you may have more disappointments.

God created us to be free beings. No matter who we are and what we do, **we must strive for what is available**.

Some things help us live God's dream, while others take us away from this dream by tempting us to pursue other dreams. The dreams of others. The dream of the world.

We must each live our own dream. We must live God's dream within us: a dream of goodness, understanding, beauty, love, compassion, mercy, patience, unfailing love, and forgiveness.

We need to learn that every difficulty in living God's dream provides us with an opportunity to get stronger, develop character, and gain new confidence.

What might be some of the opportunities the universe is providing you with to live God's dream for you? Are there any alternatives, possibilities or choices that may help you safeguard God's plan for you?

UNCOVERING THE BURIED TREASURES

Even though you may have opportunities to unleash this dream, you may still feel blocked. **Life has a way of suppressing our dreams.** These dreams can become buried under discouragement or frustrations, sin, guilt or shame, past mistakes or low self-esteem, to name a few.

Be sincere with yourself. What are you remembering right now? The hurt, the pain, what didn't work out? If this is so, try to **turn it around and seek God's dream within you once more.** Don't be scared of the pain in the process. Be aware this is a healing pain. You will be removing some dirt every time you remember this dream. You will be digging out God's dream specifically mapped out for you.

And since "The stone that the builders rejected, has become the chief cornerstone" (Psalm 118:22), I invite you to **acknowledge in writing what might have been some of the hidden treasures in your hardships**.

Do this with a sense of thanksgiving in your heart to the God that can make the wilderness blossom abundantly (Isiah 35:1). If, till now, you have not discovered the hidden treasure within that experience, write this desire as a prayer.

Accepted by God, even though a sinner

Sometimes we bring pain to ourselves by making poor choices, getting into relationships we know are not suitable for us, or maybe fighting fights that are not ours. Such experiences and sins are painful and might hinder us from acknowledging and living God's dream for us.

However, the scriptures encourage us since:

> "Neither death, nor life, nor angels, nor rulers, nor things present, nor things to come, nor powers, nor height, nor depth, nor anything else in all creation, will be able to separate us from the love of God in Christ Jesus our Lord" (Romans 8:38-39).

Encouraged by all this, I invite you to recall the experience of Saint Peter walking on water (see Matthew 14:22-33).

Notice how, when Peter first saw Jesus walking on water, he had complete trust in Him, "Lord, if it is you, command me to come to you on the water" (v.28). And to Jesus' command, "Come," "Peter got out of the boat, started walking on the water, and came toward Jesus" (v.30).

"But when he noticed the strong wind he became frightened, and, beg[an] to sink" (v.30). And as "Jesus immediately reached out his hand and caught him, saying to him, 'You of little faith, why did you doubt?'" (v.31), the same Jesus will do today for you. He will come and save you as well.

Thus, while you are aware of your sins and shortcomings, take your time now and extend your hand to the Lord by writing a prayer to entrust yourself in God's hands.

AWARE OF WHO WE ARE IN GOD

God's dream to unite you with him depends neither on you nor others but on God alone. Thus no matter what happens, God's dream of you being in union with Him is always alive and active.

Considering this, the true mark of a person pursuing God's dreams is perseverance. Thus, even though sometimes dirt gets thrown on this dream by others, including Church authorities, do not allow God's dream to get bogged down. Keep shaking off this dirt through the gift of perseverance. Keep trusting that God's Truth will soon blossom.

But the question is, **'From where can you get the strength needed for this perseverance?'**.

Under the guidance of the Holy Spirit, this **strength comes from within**. Thus, the more aware you are of your innermost profound identity in God, the easier it is for you to persevere in doing good.

So remember always that at your core, **you are a good person. You are Divine. You are the child of the living God** (cf. John 1:12).

Imprint this in yourself. Start saying positive things to yourself. Remember the greatness in you. Express with your behaviour the God within. Let the 'Christ impressed' in you be 'expressed' through your behaviour.

Do this even if your senses dictate the opposite. Do this even if you feel depressed. Do this no matter what. Collaborate with the God who dwells within you. **Keep seeking God within yourself. Keep seeking yourself in God.** Be his friend, he who is the Eternal winner.

Say to yourself, **I have the power to unite with God because "God has sent the Spirit of his Son into our hearts, crying, 'Abba! Father!'"** (Galatians 4:6).' **I have the power from on High to live this.**

I am who I am: God's Child (see John 12:36, Romans 13:12; 1 Thessalonians 5:5). **I am "the salt of the earth"** (Matthew 5:13). **I am "the light of the world"** (Matthew 5:14).

I am the "temple of the living God" (2 Corinthians 6:16). **I am part of God's dream to "Be perfect, therefore, as your heavenly Father is perfect"** (Matthew 5:48).

For this reason, through this gift of the Holy Spirit that dwells in me, I have the power to fight every evil. I can overcome every temptation. I can save my relationship. I can keep sowing the good news in the style of Christ to my family, friends, community and all the world.

What might be some of your impressions on this profound revealed identity that you have? What can you do to live according to who you are?

A RESPONSE TO A DIVINE CALL

The desire to live according to God's dream has a supernatural origin: A Divine Call.

Due to this Call (also known as the "urging grace of God"), you can live according to God's dream.

Now you understand that God's dream for you is to be united with him. Now that you know God does not care about your sins and shortcomings. God loves you unconditionally as his child.

Take your time and slowly read how the Catechism of the Catholic Church defines this Call:

> God, infinitely perfect and blessed in himself, in **a plan of sheer goodness** freely created humanity **to make every person share in his own blessed life**.
>
> For this reason, at every time and in every place, God draws close to humanity. **He calls every person to seek him, to know him, to love him with all their strength**. He calls together all people, scattered and divided by sin, into the unity of his family, the Church.

> To accomplish this, when the fullness of time had come, God sent his Son as Redeemer and Saviour. In his Son and through him, **he invites every person to become, in the Holy Spirit, his adopted children and thus heirs of his blessed life** (n.1).

A CALL FOR EVERY PERSON

This Call is for everyone. It is not limited to the baptized but is for any person of goodwill. This is because everyone possesses a rational soul and is created in God's likeness. Every person has the same nature and origin. Everyone is redeemed by Christ and enjoys the same divine calling and destiny. The second Vatican Council states:

> Every person possess a rational soul and is created in God's likeness, since they have the same nature and origin, have been redeemed by Christ and enjoy the same divine calling and destiny, the basic equality of all must receive increasingly greater recognition (*Gaudium et Spes*, 29, see also *Lumen Gentium*, 13).

For these reasons, **this Call is for you. Let nothing hinder you, neither sin nor culture nor religion**.

According to Divine Revelation, although the God who calls is one, he is nevertheless a Trinity of Persons who work together: The Father, the Son Jesus Christ and the Holy Spirit.

Take your time now, and acknowledge this Call in prayerful writing.

THE PRIVILEGED: GOD'S CHILDREN

Even though everyone is redeemed by Christ and enjoys the same divine calling and destiny, the baptized enjoy a privileged dignity (adopted children of God) and have privileged means (the sacraments) to respond to this Call. Saint Paul explains:

> Just as God chose us in Christ before the foundation of the world to be holy and blameless before him in love. He destined us for adoption as his children through Jesus Christ, according to the good pleasure of his will, to the praise of his glorious grace that he freely bestowed on us in the Beloved (Ephesians 1:4-6).

Once a person is incorporated in Christ through the sacrament of baptism, they become entitled to receive other privileged means that can make this Divine Call more personal: the sacraments.

> Incorporated in the Church **through baptism**, the faithful are destined by the baptismal character for the worship of the Christian religion; reborn as sons of God they must confess before humanity the faith which they have received from God through the Church.

They are more perfectly bound to the Church by the **sacrament of confirmation**, and the Holy Spirit endows them with special strength so that they are more strictly obliged to spread and defend the faith, both by word and by deed, as true witnesses of Christ.

Taking part in the **Eucharistic sacrifice,** which is the fount and apex of the whole Christian life, they offer the Divine Victim to God, and offer themselves along with It [...].

Strengthened in Holy Communion by the Body of Christ, they then manifest in a concrete way that unity of the people of God which is suitably signified and wondrously brought about by this most august sacrament.

Those who approach **the sacrament of Penance** obtain pardon from the mercy of God for the offence committed against Him and are at the same time reconciled with the Church, which they have wounded by their sins, and which by charity, example, and prayer seeks their conversion.

By **the sacred anointing** of the sick and the prayer of her priests the whole Church commends the sick to the suffering and glorified Lord, asking that He may lighten their suffering and save them; she exhorts them, moreover, to contribute to the welfare of the whole people of God by associating themselves freely with the passion and death of Christ.

Those of the faithful who are consecrated by **Holy Orders** are appointed to feed the Church in Christ's name with the word and the grace of God.

Finally, Christian spouses, in virtue of **the sacrament of Matrimony,** whereby they signify and partake of the mystery of that unity and fruitful love which exists between Christ and His Church, help each other to attain to holiness in their married life and in the rearing and education of their children [...].

The family is, so to speak, the domestic Church. In it parents should, by their word and example, be the first preachers of the faith to their children; they should encourage them in the vocation which is proper to each of them, fostering with special care vocation to a sacred state.

Fortified by so many and such powerful means of salvation, all the faithful, whatever their condition or state, are called by the Lord, each in his own way, to that perfect holiness whereby the Father Himself is perfect (*Lumen*

Gentium, n. 11, see also *Lumen Fidei*, 40-45, *Gaudete et Exsultate*, 14-18).

If you are baptized, take your time now to absorb this profound identity of being a true child of the living God.

Write a prayer of thanksgiving for this privilege, and in writing, ask for the gifts of wisdom and strength so that you will use these privileged and powerful means God has bestowed on you for your benefit: the sacraments. Identifying how the grace of each sacrament can help you, could be beneficial.

THE CALL OF 'GOD THE FATHER'

The Call of 'God the Father' takes form as a **"fount-like love"** (*Ad Gentes*, n. 2), which flows continuously on each human person.

As a **pilgrim toward his house** (see *Lumen Gentium*, n. 8), the response to this Call is a quest to discover, through Christ, this unconditional flowing love at any moment of your life.

This loving Father, who created all things and through whose will they continue to exist (cf. Revelations 4:11), **has a project for every single person**.

- **A project to choose life** because it belongs to him (1 Corinthians 3:22-23).
- **A project to choose the new covenant** because that which was hidden is now revealed (cf. Matthew 11.25; Luke 10:21; Colossians 1:26).
- **A project to be 'born again'** (John 3:3-8).

The human response to the Father's Call takes place with a

- **life according to the words and deeds of Christ**,
- under **the guidance of the Holy Spirit**, and
- **in the Church**.

In relation to the Father, you are called to **develop your identity as a child of God** in the child Jesus (cf. Ephesians 1:4-6).

As Jesus, in his awareness of God as Father, developed **an attitude of a real son**, you too are called to develop an attitude of a child of God. Acquired by baptism, this filial identity is developed by the following and the imitation of Christ, his Son (cf. Romans 6:4).

Because everyone is **unique**, the Father calls you for a *specific personal mission* (cf., *Evangelium vitae*, n. 78-101) that you are called to discover.

Imagine how wonderful it would be to consciously live your uniqueness as a child of God in every moment of your life. How might your life change?

Pause for a moment, and in prayer, envision the places you visit and the significant others you meet frequently and picture yourself living with this new awareness. What might be your impressions?

If you have time, express your thoughts and feelings by writing here a short letter of thanksgiving and praise to God the Father.

THE CALL OF 'JESUS CHRIST'

The Call of 'Jesus Christ' is more personal because he is both human and divine. Being the one Mediator between God and humanity (cf.1 Timothy 2:5), he who lived among us has made his Call clear through words and deeds (see *Gaudium et Spes*, n. 22). **Christ's journey on earth is like a map for you** that indicates the way to the Father (cf. John 14:6-7).

Christ **broke the chains of sin and death with which the devil wanted to bind humanity**. Having done this, Christ liberated humanity 'from' evil, sin, corruption and death 'to' a deeper union with God, our brothers, creation, and ourselves.

Christ is our **brother** (cf. John 20:17) and **friend** (cf. John 15:14-15), who identified himself with humanity except for sin (cf. Hebrews 4:15). In Christ is **the fullness of humanity**.

In response to Christ's Call, you are called to live in, with, and according to Christ to reach your fullness as a person.

You might have known Christ since when you were young. Like the disciples, you may have developed familiarity with him. The fact that you are reading this book about the dream of God is a sign that Christ is in your heart.

And as one day, Jesus asked his disciples, "Who do people say that the Son of Man is?" and "who do you say that I am?" (Matthew 16:13.15); take your time now to reply to these questions put forward by Christ himself.

Remember that to the latter question, Peter answered, "You are the Messiah, the Son of the living God" (v.16). And to this reply Jesus answered, "Blessed are you, Simon son of Jonah! For flesh and blood has not revealed this to you, but my Father in heaven" (v.17).

Thus now, in prayer—since a proper answer is a gift of God—reply to Christ's question, "who do you say that I am?" (Matthew 16:15).

The Call of the 'Holy Spirit'

The Call of the 'Holy Spirit' takes form as **a gift of the Father and of Jesus to every baptized** (see John 14,26, *Ad Gentes*, 7, 4).

As he guided Jesus in every moment of his life (cf. Luke 4:1.14; 10:21¸etc.), the Spirit continues to **guide everyone towards the Union with God**.

Jesus gave us the Holy Spirit "on the day of Pentecost so that he might continually sanctify the Church, and thus, all those who believe would have access through Christ in one Spirit to the Father" (*Lumen Gentium*, n. 2).

The Spirit is **the breath of life which gives life** (cf. Genesis 2:7). Thus, the Spirit generates and sustains you during your **journey to the union with God in Christ**.

The response to the Call of the Holy Spirit is **a life-long journey that includes moments of union with God as well as moments of ruptures due to sin**. A journey intended to lead towards heaven.

Following the example of Jesus, who allowed the Spirit to guide him throughout his life (see

Matthew 3:16, Luke 10:21, Hebrews 9:14), in **the same way, you and I must be open to the guidance of the Spirit.**

Are you aware that every good inspiration or insight you ever had was a gift of the Holy Spirit?

Take some time now and acknowledge the gifts this Spirit bestowed on you.

Acknowledge the "green pastures" the Spirit led you to and the "darkest valley" the spirit rescued you from (see Psalm 23).

Ask this Spirit to keep guiding you in every decision and situation you will find yourself in, in the future.

In Spirit and Truth

The Holy Spirit, as a guide, is also the Spirit of Truth (cf. John 15:26), **who guides the disciples into all the Truth** (cf. John 16:13).

And since this Truth can never contradict the teachings of the Church (cf. 1 Timothy 3:15), **the more you possess pure and refined knowledge of revelation, the more you can be sure of the authenticity of the promptings of the Holy Spirit** (see *Lumen Fidei*, 23-28).

Thus, to avoid false paths, one should refine the promptings of the Holy Spirit by discerning if these are in line with:

- **the words and deeds of Christ**,
- the **content and unity of all scriptures**,
- the understandings of the earliest **church fathers and mothers**,
- the **living tradition of the entire Church**,
- the **lived experience of the saints** throughout history,
- the **teachings of the present-day Magisterium**, and
- the **harmony between different elements of faith** (cf. *Dei Verbum*,n. 12).

When paying attention to the authenticity of the promptings of the Holy Spirit by seeking knowledge of revelation (as mentioned above), you must also remember that this is not merely a mathematical task that depends on your effort to obtain such knowledge.

Such discernment includes a lifelong **immersion into the mentality of Christ through an active life in the Church**, during which you learn "to think like Christ, to judge like him, to act in conformity with his commandments, and to hope as he invites us to" (*Catechesi Tradendae*, n.20).

What might be some of your impressions on the relationship between the Spirit and Truth? How might you apply this new knowledge to practice? Who may help you?

A Call within the Church

The Spirit does not only guide you to a Truth in line with revelation but leads you to live within the Church actively.

The reason is that the Church is God's home (dwelling place) on earth and is the sacrament of union with Him. Through it, God's Call for Union continues to be mediated in time (see *Lumen Gentium*, n. 1, *Lumen Fidei*, 37-39). Pope Francis explains:

> **As Christ gathers to himself all those who believe and makes them his body, so the Christian comes to see himself as a member of this body, in an essential relationship with all other believers**.
>
> The image of a body does not imply that the believer is simply one part of an anonymous whole, a mere cog in a great machine; rather, it brings out the vital union of Christ with believers and of believers among themselves (cf. *Romans* 12:4-5).
>
> **Christians are "one"** (cf. *Galatians* 3:28), **yet in a way which does not make them lose their individuality**; in service to others, they come into their own in the highest degree.

This explains why, apart from this body, outside this unity of the Church in Christ, **outside this Church** [...] **faith loses its "measure"; it no longer finds its equilibrium, the space needed to sustain itself.**

Faith is necessarily ecclesial; it is professed from within the body of Christ as a concrete communion of believers. It is against this ecclesial backdrop that faith opens the individual Christian towards all others.

Christ's word, once heard, by virtue of its inner power at work in the heart of the Christian, becomes a response, a spoken word, a profession of faith. As Saint Paul puts it: "one believes with the heart ... and confesses with the lips" (Romans 10:10).

Faith is not a private matter, a completely individualistic notion or a personal opinion: it comes from hearing, and it is meant to find expression in words and to be proclaimed [...].

Faith becomes operative in the Christian on the basis of the gift received, the love which attracts our hearts to Christ (cf. *Galatians* 5:6), **and enables us to become part of the Church's great pilgrimage through history until the end of the world** (*Lumen Fidei*, 22).

Are you aware that outside the Church, your response to God's Call loses equilibrium? Are you conscious that faith is not a private matter: you are called to live your life in response to God's Call with others?

In Harmony Between Contrasts

The Church - the place where we are called to live the response to the Call of the Father, the Son and the Holy Spirit - **is a place where harmony between contrasts is called to live together.** This is because **the Church is,**

> both human and divine, visible and yet invisibly equipped, eager to act and yet intent on contemplation, present in this world and yet not at home in it (*Sacrosanctum Concilium*, 2).

The Church is 'human' and 'divine'. She is made of humans and led by humans, all with their personalities, traits, characters, backgrounds and compromises. At the same time, it is 'divine', guided by God through the Holy Spirit, who leads the Church through these same individual members "from within" (see *Catechesi Tradendae*, n.72).

The Church is 'temporal' and 'eternal'. She 'exists in time' with all the features and constraints of any other human institution. She functions through human relationships. She needs money for her daily running, infrastructure, and communication. At the same time, the Church is 'eternal', seeking things far beyond this world (see John 17:16).

The Church is at once 'a sinner' and 'a saint'. In the Church, one member is called to help the other, especially helping those in most human and spiritual needs. It was never intended as a perfect society here on earth. In fact, in the parable of weeds among the wheat, Jesus instructed us, "Let both of them grow together until the harvest, [...since] in gathering the weeds you would uproot the wheat along with them." (Matthew 13:29-30).

Sometimes, living in the Church is not always plain sailing. It's enough to remember some alleged abuse of power, sex, and money, and one's trust in the Church, if not grounded on solid rock (see Matthew 7:24-27), will quickly be obscured.

In front of such difficulties, contaminations or scandals, as Pope Francis reminds us,

> The joy of the Gospel is such that it cannot be taken away from us by anyone or anything (cf. *Jn* 16:22).
>
> The evils of our world – and those of the Church – must not be excuses for diminishing our commitment and our fervour.

> **Let us look upon them as challenges which can help us to grow.** With the eyes of faith, we can see the light which the Holy Spirit always radiates in the midst of darkness, **never forgetting that "where sin increased, grace has abounded all the more"** (Romans 5:20) (Evangelii Gaudium, 84).

How is your experience in the Church? In what way are certain decisions of certain authorities in the Church affecting you? How is your faith affected by the good and bad behaviour of others?

What might be your contribution to the Church? How are your behaviours, choices and decisions affecting others? How might you, under the guidance of the Holy Spirit, be a force for good in the Church?

____

____

____

____

A Call with a Mission

Within the Church, you are also called to take part in the mission Christ specified for the Church:

> "Go therefore and make disciples of all nations, baptizing them in the name of the Father and of the Son and of the Holy Spirit, and teaching them to obey everything that I have commanded you" (Matthew 28:19-20).

Pope Francis reminds every baptized person of this mission by stating,

> **In virtue of their baptism, all the members of the People of God have become missionary disciples** (cf. Mt 28:19).
>
> All the baptized, whatever their position in the Church or their level of instruction in the faith, are agents of evangelization, and it would be insufficient to envisage a plan of evangelization to be carried out by professionals while the rest of the faithful would simply be passive recipients.
>
> **The new evangelization calls for personal involvement on the part of each of the baptized.** Every Christian is challenged, here and now, to be actively engaged in

> evangelization; indeed, anyone who has truly experienced God's saving love does not need much time or lengthy training to go out and proclaim that love (*Evangelii Gaudium*, n.120).

Thus, through this mission, the circle of God's Call for You will be closed since you are called to share with others what you have received from God the Father, the Son and the Holy Spirit.

Are you aware of this mandatory Call to evangelize? How can you become more aware of this responsibility? How might you be a better witness of God with your family members, co-workers, in politics, and in society?

According to one's gifts and duties

> **Every person must walk unhesitatingly according to their gifts and duties in the path of living faith, which arouses hope and works through charity** (*Lumen Gentium*, 41).

These words from the Dogmatic Constitution on the Church, '*Lumen Gentium*', remind us that even though everyone is called to evangelize, our gifts, duties, and state of life – whether ordained or married – direct us to a specific mission.

Below is an overview offered by Vatican II of the essence of each specific Call. *Take some time now, and reflect on your particular Call of evangelization.*

> **The shepherds of Christ's flock** must holily and eagerly, humbly and courageously carry out their ministry in imitation of the eternal high Priest, the Shepherd and Guardian of our souls [...].
>
> **Married couples and Christian parents** should follow their own proper path (to holiness) by faithful love. They should sustain one another in grace throughout the entire length of their lives.

They should embue their offspring, lovingly welcomed as God's gift, with Christian doctrine and the evangelical virtues [...].

Those who are weighed down with poverty, infirmity and sickness, as well as those who must bear various hardships or who suffer persecution for justice's sake—may they all know they are united with the suffering Christ in a special way for the salvation of the world [...].

Finally, **all Christ's faithful**, whatever be the conditions, duties and circumstances of their lives—and indeed through all these, will daily increase in holiness if they receive all things with faith from the hand of their heavenly Father and if they cooperate with the divine will.

In this temporal service, **they will manifest to all humanity the love with which God loved the world** (*Lumen Gentium*, 41).

A PROPER RESPONSE TO GOD'S CALL

The desire to live according to God's dream has a supernatural 'origin' (a Divine Call) **and a supernatural 'aim'** (union with God now and for all eternity). **Thus, you need supernatural means to achieve it.**

According to John of the Cross, the appropriate attitude to this response is **an attitude of faith, hope and love** (Ascent 2,8,2-3).

The reason is that these so-called theological virtues

> *"have the function of withdrawing the soul from all that is less than God. They consequently have the mission of joining it with God"* (The Dark Night, II, 22, 11-12).

This is not a difficult task since these virtues relate directly to God and are infused in you through baptism to help you live God's dream for you (See *Catechism of the Catholic Church*, n. 1812-1813).

Thus, for the discovery and actualization of God's dream, it is necessary to:

1. collaborate with the grace that originates in the Call of God for Union, and
2. use *supernatural means* as a response, namely, *the theological virtues of faith, hope and love.*

An Attitude of Faith, Hope and Love

The question now is: What do these virtues mean in practice?

The virtue of faith enables you to believe in God and freely commit yourself to him. It empties your thoughts from their natural understanding and leads you to look at life through the eyes and mentality of God.

The virtue of hope slowly withdraws your desires to earthly possessions. Hope helps you focus on the ultimate goal: the union with God in Christ. Through hope, you can desire and wait for eternal union with God.

The virtue of love empties and annihilates your affections and appetites from that which is not God and centres them on him alone through love. Through the virtue of love, you can live Christ's command to love God above all things and your neighbour as yourself for the love of God (cf., Matthew 22:37-39; Mark 12:30-31; Luke 10:27-29).

Take your time now to acknowledge these virtues infused in you through creation and baptism. Observe how they have helped you throughout your life without you even knowing it, and write a prayer asking God to strengthen you in these virtues.

A UNIQUE AND PERSONAL MISSION

While living God's dream for you, you will find that the Father wants to trust you with a particular mission here on earth: **God's unique dream for you!**

It is a personal mission that activates God's dream in you for the good of others. This personal mission **highlights the fact that you are a unique person**. It immerses you in God's dream for humanity.

This personal mission mustn't be confused with one's state of life (ordained or married) or vocation. It's not one's profession or job. It's not, at least in most cases, a 'spectacular enterprise' or a perpetual 'painful Calvary'.

This particular mission is discovered in time by an individual through the different experiences, situations and knowledge that one acquires.

These 'particular missions' allow Christ to live in the world in different dimensions. As Saint Paul states:

> Now you are the body of Christ and individually members of it. And God has appointed in the

> church first apostles, second prophets, third teachers; then deeds of power, then gifts of healing, forms of assistance, forms of leadership, various kinds of tongues. Are all apostles? Are all prophets? (1 Corinthians 12:27-30).

Thus, **God appoints personal missions for the service of the whole Church.** No one mission is better than the others, but each one is important for the rest since,

> "For just as the body is one and has many members, and all the members of the body, though many, are one body, so it is with Christ" (1 Corinthians 12:12).

Have you discovered your personal mission yet? In which direction do you feel the Spirit is guiding you? Which episodes of Christ's life are moving your heart? If you have an indication, please write it down as a prayer. If not, ask him once again for a sign.

Try not to let this mission be engulfed by too much thought, obsessions, or excessive internal dialogue.

What might be the role of your tiny dot in God's grand design? What might be the role that ONLY

YOU can play in his magnificent and glorious dream for humanity?

In God's timing

Sometimes, when God trusts us with a personal mission, we do not see the outcome immediately. When this happens, we might feel frustrated. But **our timing is not always God's timing.**

For us, waiting can be a significant challenge. We may feel we have lost control. However, God can use this time to teach us humility and obedience. He can use this time to help us grow in patience or to develop a child-like trust in him. God can use this time to show us that it is his dream, his project, not ours!

From the experiences narrated in the scriptures, one can learn that **God is never in a hurry**. For example:

- David had to wait for about **fifteen years** from the time Samuel anointed him to the time he became king over Judah (see 2 Samuel 2:1-5:5).
- Joseph waited **twenty-two years** before helping his family. These included thirteen years of slavery and prison, seven years of plenty, and two years of famine (see Genesis 45:11).

- Moses waited **forty years** in Midian before delivering Israel (Exodus 2:11-3:22).
- "Jesus was about **thirty years** old when he began his work" (Luke 3:23).

All this teaches us that we must walk by faith, not sight, when relating to God's dream. Faith can help us obtain the sight of God, which sees far and beyond all we can see. When we question God's timing, **we might be trying to fit our plans and purposes into God's far superior timeline**. We need to remind ourselves:

> "For my thoughts are not your thoughts, nor are your ways my ways, says the LORD. For as the heavens are higher than the earth, so are my ways higher than your ways and my thoughts than your thoughts" (Isiah 55:8-9).

Waiting on the Lord can take us deeper into his mystery, where you can experience his power and glory. Take, for instance, the story of Lazarus (John 11). Initially, Jesus gets word that his friend Lazarus is critically ill. Contrary to what we might have done, he doesn't run to heal him but stays put without any reaction for two days before leaving.

When Jesus arrived in Bethany, Lazarus had been dead and decaying for four days in the tomb. However, what was initially perceived as an unwarranted delay, was intended to show everyone that Jesus is not only able to heal the sick but even resurrect the dead.

Waiting is also a natural process. Nature teaches us that there is a season to reap the fruit and a season to prune. There is a time to act and a time to sleep and rest. One can observe such cycles through the actualization of one's personal mission.

The good news is that as an orange tree produces oranges as fruit, so does an apple tree generates apples and not the other way round; **what God plants in your heart will one day bear fruit in its time** since "the one who began a good work in you will continue to complete" (Philippians 1:6).

And **the fruit will not be yours, but God's**, as Saint Paul explains: "I planted, Apollos watered, but God gave the growth" (1 Corinthians 3:6). And the fruit you will reap will be much greater than you have ever thought or imagined.

> "Wait for the LORD; be strong, and let your heart take courage; wait for the LORD!" (Psalm 27:14).

Have you ever waited for the Lord? What might be some of your impressions, thoughts and feelings on God's timing?

Consolation vs Desolation

The delay in God's timing might make you anxious, angry, doubtful, or resentful. When this happens, you must distinguish between experienced consolations and desolations.

St. Ignatius of Loyola defines these in his discernment of the spirit rules as follows:

Consolation is,

> when any interior movement is produced in the soul which leads her to be inflamed with the love of her creator and Lord [...]
>
> when a person sheds tears which lead to the love of our Lord [and ...]
>
> every increase in faith hope and charity, to all interior happiness which calls and attracts to heavenly things and to the salvation of the soul, **leaving the soul quiet and at peace in her Creator the Lord"** (Spiritual Exercises, n.316).

Desolation is the opposite. It contains attributes,

> such as the darkness of the soul, disturbance in it, movement to low and earthly things, disquiet from various agitations and temptations,

> moving to lack of confidence, without hope, without love, finding oneself totally slothful, tepid, sad, and, as if separated from one's Creator and Lord (Spiritual Exercises, n.317).

It is important to note that **desolation is not typical of an authentic spiritual journey.**

To help you rid yourself of useless desolations, I will list some possible causes of desolation and the cure for each.

The causes of desolation can be:

- A **'personal decision'** leading to sin, error, fault, or lack of self-care.
- **'God',** to teach us something, to make us aware of any darkness that has taken root in our lives, or to remind us that consolation is a gift from him, not something we have earned for ourselves.
- **'The evil spirit'** can also create disturbances and impediments through temptations, insinuations, and occasionally through vexations, oppressions, physical attacks, and diabolical possession.
- **Poor physical or mental health**

- **Toxic environments** like homes or places of work in which one lives with excessive unhealthy anxiety, sadness, obsessions, hatred, envy, fornication, jealousy, rage, sinful sexuality, harmful friendships, divisions, spells, blasphemy, witchcraft and the occult.

The therapy is:

- If a personal decision, **convert and turn back to God**.

- If God, **persevere.**

- If an evil spirit, **react and defend yourself.**

- If you have poor health, **have patience and learn how to wait**.

- If the fault is found in your environment, **try to change it by going elsewhere. If change is not possible, then rely more on God's protection.**

When experiencing desolation, it is crucial to ask the Holy Spirit for the **gift of wisdom** to learn the cause of such desolations and the **gift of strength** to carry out the therapy needed.

What may be some of your impressions about the above?

What might be some of the causes of your desolations?

ALWAYS IN A PROCESS OF CONVERSION

Whatever this dream, whatever the timing, you will always be in a 'process of conversion'—always trying. You ought to constantly adapt to new circumstances.

The word 'conversion' means 'turning back'. **Turning back to who you are: a creature created in the image of God, a child of the living God**.

Turning back to God is a process that happens throughout life. It is not a single event. Through conversion, you will **express (bring out) by your behaviour the Christ which is already impressed in you through creation and baptism**.

The need for this 'turning back' ('conversion') to God in Christ comes because of the 'sin' of our first parents and its effect on humanity. This sin does not separate us from God since in Him we live and move (cf. Acts 17:28); however, it lessens the perfect intimacy.

In this context, God chooses to repair this damage caused by sin through the intervention of a mediator: the incarnation of his only-begotten

Son, and declares him to be the only perfect Mediator of the new covenant.

In practice, this happens **through a personal encounter with Christ.** Like Zacchaeus, who converted just by meeting Jesus (see Luke 19:1-10), today, **you can meet Jesus and convert while reading the Gospels**.

This encounter is possible due to Christ's promise:

> "the Advocate, the Holy Spirit, whom the Father will send in my name, will teach you everything, and remind you of all that I have said to you" (John 14:26).

In this phrase, the verb 'remind,' in Hebrew, 'zakar,' derived from 'zikkaron' the 'memory' of Easter, does not only mean to commemorate but to live a right-now experience.

During this prayer, you do not need to make big efforts to encounter Christ. You do not need to 'run ahead' and 'climb trees' as Zacchaeus did (cf. Luke 19:4). You must simply **acknowledge God's real presence within yourself and stay in his presence**.

You must simply seek yourself in God and seek God within yourself (cf. Teresa of Avila, Poems, 8). This relationship is always possible even if you are in mortal sin (cf., John of the Cross, *The Spiritual Canticle*, Stanza 1, 8). The encounter with Christ will transform your mind and heart.

Where you aware that conversion is a life-long process to express (bring out) by your behaviour the Christ which is already impressed in you? Are you aware that this is a life-long process? Since this conversion depends on your relationship with God, entrust yourself to him by writing a prayer that expresses your new understanding of conversion.

THE NEED TO DISCERN GOD'S WILL

What is discernment? We can describe discernment as **the ability to stay in a prayerful thinking process to determine the difference between right and wrong, truth and error, and between good and evil in the form of good**.

There are also **different types of discernment**.

- **In particular times:** when the person enters into an intense time of discernment, to take a challenging decision in front of God, the Church and Society.
- **Daily**: when one seeks God's Will in everyday situations.
- **Communitarian**: when God's Will is discerned according to one's conscience with others. For example, when it occurs within the context of a family, group, parish, diocese, or the entire Church.

In living the dream of God, you are called to engage in all these types of discernment.

Discernment is a gift from God through the Holy Spirit (see 1 Corinthians 2:12–15). "He gives wisdom to the wise and knowledge to the discerning" (Daniel 2:21). This is a gift that we should continually ask for (see James 1:4). It is a gift that he likes to give to those who trust in him (Proverbs 3:5-6).

Familiarity with scriptures leads to a better grasp of the thought of God since,

> the word of God is living and active, sharper than any two-edged sword, piercing until it divides soul from spirit, joints from marrow; it is able to judge the thoughts and intentions of the heart (Hebrews 4:12).

Discernment **is not an easy task**.

> **Discernment involves hard work.** According to the Bible, we do not find set before us, pre-packaged, the life we are to live. No! **We have to decide it all the time, according to the reality that comes**.
>
> **God invites us to evaluate and choose**: He created us free and wants us to exercise our freedom. Therefore, discerning is *demanding* [...].
>
> **Discernment is demanding but indispensable for living**. It requires that I know myself, that I know what is good for me here and now. Above

> all, **it requires a filial relationship with God** (Pope Francis, 31 August 2022).

The question we need to face here is, ***What might I do to learn if I am on the right track or on the wrong path?*** What might be some of the criteria leading to proper discernment?

Key discernment criteria

One of the main criteria in discerning God's will is **an assessment of the fruits** since:

> **every good tree bears good fruit, but the bad tree bears bad fruit.** A good tree cannot bear bad fruit, nor can a bad tree bear good fruit (Matthew 7:17-20).

Saint Paul offers us a thorough distinction between the fruits of the flesh and those of the spirit:

> **The works of the flesh are obvious:** fornication, impurity, licentiousness, idolatry, sorcery, enmities, strife, jealousy, anger, quarrels, factions, dissensions, envy, drunkenness, carousing, and things like these [...].
>
> **By contrast, the fruit of the Spirit is** love, joy, peace, patience, kindness, generosity,

> faithfulness, gentleness, and self-control (Galatians 5:16-25).

Another biblical passage that introduces us easily to the practical process of discernment is Romans 12:2:

> "*do not be conformed to this world, but be transformed by the renewing of your minds, so that you may discern what is the will of God–what is good and acceptable and perfect*" (Romans 12:2).

In this exhortation, there is an **order** to be obeyed and consists of being "*transformed by the renewing of your minds,*" an **aim** to be reached, "*discern what is the will of God,*" and a **great enemy** for this renewing process, "*do not be conformed to this world.*"

The **alternative model** for transformed living is not specified here, but **that Christ was both the pattern and source of this renewal and transformation is clear enough** and had been indicated with sufficient clarity in chapters 6–8 of this same letter.[1]

---

[1] These distinctions are found in, James D. G. DUNN, *Word Biblical Commentary: Romans 9-16*, Vol. 38B, Word Biblical Commentary, Word Incorporated, Dallas 1988, p. 715ff.

Finally, one needs to be aware that **different spirits might be involved in your thinking and decision-making regarding God's will for you.** Saint John and Saint Paul exhort:

> Beloved, do not believe every spirit, but test the spirits to see whether they are from God (1 John 4:1).

> Do not despise prophecies, but test everything; hold fast to what is good; abstain from every form of evil (1 Thessalonians 5:20-21).

This is the most sensitive part of the discernment process since **while it is easy to distinguish between the good and the bad, it is not that easy to differentiate between the good and the evil under the form of good**.

On one side, there is always God's Spirit, the Holy Spirit, the Spirit of Truth, and close to it, there is always our own egoistic Human Spirit and The Evil Spirit. The latter always aims to deceive us, pretending to be the good spirit, to destroy our life here on earth and in the afterlife through eternal damnation.

DIVINE, HUMAN AND DIABOLICAL SPIRITS

Here are some signs that can help identify the different types of spirits that might be guiding you.[2] A deeper explanation of these signs is offered in the third book in this series, 'Guided by the Holy Spirit'.

The Signs of the **'Divine Spirit'** are:

- Conformity with revelation.
- Promotion of fraternal charity.
- Humility: being in the Truth.
- Docility – obedience
- Moderation and equilibrium.
- Peace and serenity.

The signs of the **'Human spirit'** are:

- Mental egocentrism – judge and evaluate according to one's interests and tastes.
- Existential egocentrism – to act at any cost to satisfy one's own needs and interests.
- Lack of docility – obedience.
- Seeking compensation.

---

[2] These signs are taken from Benito GOYA, *Luce e guida nel cammino. Manuale di direzione spirituale*, Mauali, EDB, Bologna 2004, pp. 145-171.

The signs of a **'Diabolical spirit'** are:

- A tendency to falsity
- Spirit of pride and rebellion.
- Spirit of discord
- Lack of internal peace.

In discerning God's dream, one must strive to be guided solely by the Divine Spirit. This does not mean that one is immune to being deceived.

One must remember that as "where sin increased, grace abounded all the more" (Romans 5:20), it is also true that where grace abounds, the more furious, cunning and deceptive becomes the evil one. Together with this deception from the evil spirit, we need to be aware that our human nature also belongs to this world rather than solely to God.

What might be some of your impressions on the criteria for discernment? Do you observe any signs in yourself or others of the spirits, as described earlier?

Living what lacks from Christ's passion

Living God's dream is the most beautiful thing that we can experience. It can bring us an ever-ending joy: eternal joy. However, **this does not mean that we won't encounter difficult moments**.

For Christians, the cross is the means to reach union with God. Christ told us,

> "If any want to become my followers, let them deny themselves and take up their cross daily and follow me. For those who want to save their life will lose it, and those who lose their life for my sake will save it" (Luke 9:23-24).

Saint John Paul II, in a General Audience on 17 August 1988, explained,

> "In human life, suffering signifies a test of the human Spirit's strength. Such a test has a 'liberating' significance: it liberates the Spirit's hidden strengths and allows them to appear. At the same time, it becomes an occasion of interior purification.

> The words of the parable of the vine and the branches told by Jesus are relevant here, especially when he presents the Father as the one who cultivates the vineyard: 'Every branch of mine that does bear fruit he prunes that it may bear more fruit' (John 15:2).
>
> That fruit depends on remaining (like a branch) in Christ the vine, in his redemptive sacrifice, because 'apart from him we can do nothing' (cf. John 15:5) [...]. In this way the Christian's gradual transformation according to the model of Christ is accomplished."

Thus carrying our cross, following the example of Christ, **we are enabled to remove that which is not Christ in us**. More than this, carrying the cross **allows us to complete what "is lacking in Christ's afflictions for the sake of his body, that is, the church"** (Colossians 1:24).

Through this purification due to the will and strength of God and Christ's passion, we can one day say with Saint Paul, "I have been crucified with Christ, and **it is no longer I who live, but it is Christ who lives in me**. And the life I now live in the flesh I live by faith in the Son of God, who loved me and gave himself for me" (Galatians 2:19-20).

This union with God in Christ that comes out of the purification of the cross makes enduring such a burden worth it since, in relation to this union, everything else is "rubbish" (cf. Philippians 3:7-8).

Knowing that such a prize is awaiting us, we have nothing else to do other than to **"Fight the good fight of the faith"** (1 Timothy 6:12), in order to

> **"Let the same mind be in you that was in Christ Jesus**, who, though he was in the form of God, did not regard equality with God as something to be exploited, but emptied himself, taking the form of a slave, being born in human likeness. And being found in human form, he humbled himself and became obedient to the point of death—even death on a cross" (Philippians 2:5-8).

Have you ever felt the burden of the cross? What was/is your experience? How might the above information alter your perception of such difficult moments?

You can use this space to write a prayer regarding some of your daily crosses, asking the Holy Spirit for wisdom and strength.

Or *you can simply say with* Christ, "Father, if you are willing, remove this cup from me; yet, not my will but yours be done" (Luke 22:42).

Or you may feel that the serenity prayer suits you most:

> God grant me the SERENITY to accept the things I cannot change, the COURAGE to change the things I can, and the WISDOM to know the difference.

GROWING IN LOVE WITH GOD AND OTHERS

In living God's dream, you need to start expressing in your own words and deeds the good news, love, and happiness to your family, friends, co-workers and all the people surrounding you.

Like the sower in the parable (Matthew 13:1-23), you are called to spread the Good News everywhere. Planting even in the path where the seed might be lost. You must be **abundant in your goodness**, like your Father who is in heaven.

Your eternal union with God depends on this. Listen to the criteria by which you are going to be judged at the end of time:

> "Come, you that are blessed by my Father, inherit the kingdom prepared for you from the foundation of the world; for I was hungry and you gave me food, I was thirsty and you gave me something to drink, I was a stranger and you welcomed me, I was naked and you gave me clothing, I was sick and you took care of me, I was in prison and you visited me" (Matthew 25:34-36).

Like Jesus, who gave his life "out of love for the Father" (John 14:30; see 10:17) and "out of love for us" (John 1:11; 11:51-52; etc...), in living God's dream, you ought to do the same. While not accepting any compromise with injustice or abuse, with the help of the Holy Spirit, **you must keep striving to grow in this love**.

If you see your daily behaviour, do you see yourself expressing the Good News? Is your behaviour conducive to a favourable judgment at the end of your life? What might be some of the strategies/decisions you can consider to extend and strengthen your love towards others?

BEING A GOOD EXAMPLE TO OTHERS

The actualization of God's dream is not a self-enclosed or narcissistic spiritual activity but is lived in the Church and for the service of the Church, society and the world. This is because

> The one whom the Father has sent to do his will (cf. John 5:36-38; 6:38-40; 7:16-18) draws us to himself and makes us part of his life and mission. The Spirit of the Risen Lord empowers us to proclaim the word everywhere by the witness of our lives.
>
> This was experienced by the first Christian community, which saw the word spread through preaching and witness (cf. Acts 6:7).
>
> Here we can think in particular of the life of the Apostle Paul, a man completely caught up by the Lord (cf. *Philippians* 3:12) – "it is no longer I who live, but Christ who lives in me" (*Galatians* 2:20) – and by his mission: "woe to me if I do not proclaim the Gospel!" (*1 Corintians* 9:16) – (Benedict XVI, *Verbum Domini*, 91).

This is a call for everyone, and thus for **every person according to his or her own gifts** (cf. Romans 12:6), **opportunity, ability, charism and**

ministry (cf. 1 Corinthians 3:10) **has to make an effort to be witness to Christ with confidence and constancy** (cf. Acts 4:13, 29, 31; 9:27, 28; 13:46; 14:3; 19:8; 26:26; 28:31; 1 Thessalonians 2:2; 2 Corinthians 3:12; 7:4; Philippians 1:20; Ephesians 3:12; 6:19, 20).

This could happen through us giving a good example to others (1 Thessalonians 1:6; 2:14; 3:7, 9; Philippians 3:17; 1 Corinthians 4:16–17; 11:1; Hebrews 6:12; 13:7), **as well as by an organized pastoral action.**

What might be some of your impressions about how you practice your love towards God and others (family, significant others, community, society)? If you watch the movie of a typical day of yours, do you see yourself leaving a trail of good or bad examples? Do you leave Christ imprinted in your actions?

In the environment, God chose for you.

No one chose to be born. No one decided to be born now. No one selected the place where one was born. No one selected the environment. No one selected one's childhood friends or one's primary education.

There is no ideal situation. The poor might complain that they are poor. The rich might see their richness as a disadvantage as well. As you grow older, you can then start choosing. You can be attentive to specific opportunities. You can begin to decide.

Now, being aware that "No one can believe alone, just as no one can live alone" (Catechism, 166), I invite you to **commit yourself to be surrounded with happy and wonderful people that, like you, are striving to discover and live God's dream for themselves.** Let them be your example and support like the first Christians who supported each other in faith (see Philippians 3:17; 2 Thessalonians 3:7, 9; Hebrews 6:12; 13:7).

Fill your mind with the examples of the saints since:

> "When we look at the lives of those who have faithfully followed Christ, we are inspired with a new reason for seeking the City that is to come (cf. Hebrews 13:14; 11:10) and at the same time we are shown the safest path by which among the vicissitudes of this world, in keeping with the state in life and condition proper to each of us, we will be able to arrive at perfect union with Christ, that is, perfect holiness" (*Lumen Gentium*, 57).

God's dream in you is like a seed, full of gifts, talents, and potential. But if you plant yourself in unhealthy soil; if you hang around friends that compromise you with the mentality of the world (cf. Romans 12:2), that can pull you down; if you regularly feed your mind on the internet with negative news or negative behaviours; if you live in an environment that is limited to people that continuously suppress you, tell you what you cannot become instead of who you could be: **it is difficult to see the growth that should be yours.**

So take your time now to acknowledge and name the opportunities, people, experiences, knowledge, and communities available to you as a resource for this conversion process, leading you to recognize and share God's Dream.

People:

Places:

Environments:

Knowledge (internet, books...):

Taking Care of the Temple of the Spirit

To live God's dream fully, you must also care for the Temple of the Spirit: your physical body (see 1 Corinthians 6:19). You need to take care of it since it belongs to God:

> "You do not belong to yourself, for God bought you with a high price. So, you must honour God with your body" (see 1 Corinthians 6:19-20).

We need to take care of it since there will be a time when "the Spirit is willing, but the flesh [will be] weak." (see Matthew 26:41). We must take care of it since this body is the only one we got.

This point might sound ridiculous, but **sometimes we live as if we have bodies to spare**. When the one we have is worn out, we don't have a replacement until the day of resurrection!

Moreover, **poor discipline relating to our bodies is a bad witness.** It's hard to advise people to be disciplined in their faith and prayer when they can look at us and see we ourselves are undisciplined in our physical activity eating and drinking. A lack of effort in one area of life is often symptomatic of problems in other areas. Moreover, **better health translates into more energy to live God's Dream!**

Taking all this into consideration, let me now acknowledge the state of my health and plan on how I may better take care of this temple that God has entrusted me with.

Balance: How is my daily routine? Am I taking moments of rest during the week and extended ones during the year?

Do I live a balanced life with time for myself, God, my family, and the community?

Diet: Do I have a healthy relationship with food and drink? Who can help me? What may be improved?

Exercise: How is my exercise regime? Who can help me further improve my performance?

In His Presence Day and Night

Even though the actualization of God's dream does not happen without our free collaboration to 'accept' or 'deny' this gift, His grace generates' a free response and 'sustains' it. Thus, we must continually be in union with him to actualize this dream. **Like a bulb that cannot emit light if not connected with electricity, the same holds true for the Christian, who, if not connected to Christ, cannot be the "light of the world"** (John 8:12). Jesus was clear:

> "Abide in me as I abide in you. Just as the branch cannot bear fruit by itself unless it abides in the vine, neither can you unless you abide in me. I am the vine, you are the branches.
>
> Those who abide in me and I in them bear much fruit, because apart from me you can do nothing. Whoever does not abide in me is thrown away like a branch and withers; such branches are gathered, thrown into the fire, and burned.
>
> If you abide in me, and my words abide in you, ask for whatever you wish, and it will be done for you. My Father is glorified by this, that you bear much fruit and become my disciples.

As the Father has loved me, so I have loved you; abide in my love. If you keep my commandments, you will abide in my love, just as I have kept my Father's commandments and abide in his love. I have said these things to you so that my joy may be in you, and that your joy may be complete.

This is my commandment, that you love one another as I have loved you. No one has greater love than this, to lay down one's life for one's friends. You are my friends if you do what I command you. I do not call you servants any longer, because the servant[does not know what the master is doing; but I have called you friends, because I have made known to you everything that I have heard from my Father.

You did not choose me but I chose you. And I appointed you to go and bear fruit, fruit that will last, so that the Father will give you whatever you ask him in my name. I am giving you these commands so that you may love one another" (John 15:1-17).

Now, since Christ is present for us all the time, **every moment in which we are not living in his presence is a moment taken away from him.** John of the Cross explains,

> "The entire world is not worthy of man's thought, for this belongs to God alone; any thought, therefore, not centred on God is stolen from him" (*Maxims of Love*, 37).

It is clear then that for us **to live in the presence of Christ, we need, first of all, to have a 'desire' to so live in his presence**. John of the Cross continues to explain that,

> "when the soul desires God fully, it then possesses him whom it loves. [...] *the more the soul desires God, the more it possesses him*, and the possession of God delights and satisfies it. [...] the greater the soul's desire, the greater will be its satisfaction and delight rather than its suffering and pain" (*The living flame of Love*, 3, 23).

Once this desire is present, **the primary means that might help us to stay in his presence are**:

- **Recollection**. Dedicating time for God alone.
- **Prayer**. The most profound and most direct meeting with God.
- **The Eucharist**, receiving Communion and adoration.
- **Listening to the Word of God.**

While these are the primary means, other exercises could help to stay in God's presence. These include:

- **Pious *invocations* and *ejaculatory* prayers,** which, when regularly practised, remind us of the presence of God in us.
- ***Spiritual communions,*** which remind us of the presence of Jesus and render present his redeeming sacrifice.
- **Offering every action** to God.
- Grow in the habit of **seeing in the people we meet daily, the Christ who lives in them or wishes to live in them**.
- ***Living in a relationship with God* through the concrete realities of our day**.
- Constantly **asking**:
    - *What might the Father's Plan be for me?*
    - *Where is the Holy Spirit taking my life?*
    - *What would Jesus think, feel or do?*
- **Observing God's work in the world.**
- **Freeing myself from all that closes my heart from acquiring God's presence.**
- **Acting creatively in love to become more aware of God's constant presence.**

While looking at your typical day and typical week, identify ways and means to remain in God's presence.

Commit yourself NOW!

Upon discovering this dream, your life will never be the same again! Today is the beginning of the rest of your life! Have you ever seen your life through God's eyes like this before?

Going back to your environment could be a little frightening. But **the Holy Spirit who dwells in you can make a way where there seems to be no way. So be courageous! Be passionate about living God's dream! Allow the Spirit who dwells in you to help you think outside the box and be creative so that the Father's Will for you will be actualized.**

If you would like more help in this regard, keep in touch with the God Mediation Publications *since we are planning to support your journey with the following books:*

- Finding yourself in God, *on the identity as children of God*
- Doing the will of the Father
- Following and imitating Christ
- Guided by the Holy Spirit
- Living in the Church
- Serving others while caring for nature

In the meantime, focus on who you are. Live the dream. **Live God's Dream within you!** Trust him, and he will do the rest.

Allow God to continue to live in this world throughout your entire being. Through your hands. Through your mouth. Through your eyes. Your Creativity.

Live God's Eternal Dream in you! Your life now, as it is, is the only chance you have! Just keep fighting, no matter what, to **LIVE GOD'S DREAM FOR YOU!**

A FINAL PRAYER

Usually, books come to an end by the conclusion. However, since this is a practical book on LIVING THE DREAM OF GOD, I invite you to conclude this journal by relating to the God who aims to realize his dreams through you.

In practice, this prayer can help you summarize the spiritual movements experienced while reading this book and reinforce the promptings of the Holy Spirit through a practical and focused action plan. In doing so, please pay attention not to render this final prayer to an intellectual endeavour. Aim to relate to God at every step.

Aware of all this, **start this final prayer by asking for the guidance of the Holy Spirit to help you identify and name the main insights that spoke to your mind and heart while reading and praying with this book.**

Note with particular attention the experienced spiritual consolations. It could be helpful to look again at each page of this book to identify the most profound spiritual movements experienced while reading and journaling.

Do you consider these insights merely human thoughts, or can you consider them **a gift from God,** who spoke to you while reading this book?

What comparisons might you make between what you knew about God, yourself, others and the Church and what you have just learned?

My general idea of God was

Now I view God as

Before reading 'Living the dream of God', I used to see myself as

Now I see myself as

My ideas of others and the Church were

Now I see others and the Church as

While being aware that discovering and actualizing God's dream for you is a lifelong endeavour, what were the main hunches and intuitions that emerged while reading this book regarding this dream?

Which spirit (human, Divine or diabolical) could be the guiding force of your actual desires?

How do you react when there is a dissonance between your timing and God's?

Which insights do you feel the Holy Spirit is guiding you to apply after closing this book? What do you need to be mindful of to employ this in practice? Please ask for the gifts of knowledge and wisdom to choose which is best for you according to God's plan.

How do you know that this effort will help you grow in love towards God and others within the Church?

While aware of all the above, ask the Holy Spirit to help you write **God's Dream for you in one statement**.

How do you know that this is possible?

What might be some of the strategies or decisions you are considering to keep this dream alive and active?

How and when will you evaluate whether or not God's dream is kept alive and active in you?

To keep God's dream alive and active for you, others and the Church in your everyday life, what do you consider is the most important thing you need to pay attention to?

Finally, while being aware that "Unless the LORD builds the house, those who build it labor in vain (Psalm 127:1), and aware also that "the heavenly Father give the Holy Spirit to those who ask him" (Luke 11:13): conclude this prayer journey by asking God the Father to bestow on you the Holy Spirit, so that, following the example of Christ, God's dream for you will be actualized.

Write this in the form of an act of trust in God and in his timing, and while doing so, be aware that "the one who began a good work in you will continue to complete it" (Philippians 1:6).

Bibliography

1. Holy Scripture

THE HOLY BIBLE, *New Revised Standard Version*, Thomas Nelson Publishers, Nashville TN 1989.

2. Church Documents

BENEDICT XVI, Post-Synodal Apostolic Exhortation, *Verbum Domini*, 30 September 2010.

CATECHISM OF THE CATHOLIC CHURCH, 11 October 1992, Doubleday, New York NY, 1995.

CONGREGATION FOR THE CLERGY, *General Directory for Catechesis*, 17 August 1997, LEV, Vatican City 1997.

FRANCIS, Apostolic Exhortation on the call to holiness in today's world, *Gaudete et exsultate*, 19 March 2018.

_____. Apostolic Exhortation on the Proclamation of the Gospel in Today's World, *Evangelii Gaudium*, 24 November 2013.

_____. General Audience, Catechesis On Discernment: 1. *What does it mean to discern?*, 31 August 2022.

_____. Encyclical Letter, *Fratelli tutti*, 3 October 2020.

_____. Encyclical Letter, *Laudato si'*, 24 May 2015.

_____. Encyclical Letter, *Lumen fidei*, 29 June 2013.

_____. Post-Synodal Exhortation to Young People and to the entire People of God, *Christus vivit*, 25 March 2019.

_____.Post-Synodal Apostolic Exhortation on love in the family, *Amoris laetitia*, 19 March 2016.

JOHN PAUL II, Apostolic Exhortation, *Catechesi Tradendae*, 16 October 1979.

_____. Encyclical Letter, *Dominum et Vivificantem*, 18 May 1986.

_____. Encyclical Letter, *Redemptor Hominis*, 4 March 1979.

_____. Encyclical Letter, *Veritatis Splendor*, 6 August 1993.

_____. *Jesus is our model*, General audience, 17 August 1988; printed in Italian in, Insegniamenti, Vol. XI, 3 1988 (July – October), LEV, Vatican City 1991, pp. 394-398.

_____. Post-synodal Apostolic Exhortation, *Christifedelis Laici*, 30 December 1989.

PONTIFICAL BIBLICAL COMMISSION, *The Bible and Morality. Biblical roots of Christian conduct*, 11 May 2008, LEV, Vatican City 2008.

_____. *Instruction on Scripture and Christology*, 6 January 1984; English translation in Joseph A. FITZMYER, *Scripture and Christology: a statement of the Biblical Commission with a commentary*, Paulist Press, New York NY, 1986.

_____. *The Interpretation of the Bible in the Church*, 15 April 1993, Pauline, Boston 1993.

PONTIFICAL COUNCIL FOR CULTURE and PONTIFICAL COUNCIL FOR RELIGIOUS DIALOGUE, *Jesus Christ the bearer of the water of life. A Christian reflection on the New Age*, 02 March 2003, Pauline, Boston 2003.

VATICAN COUNCIL II, Decree on the missionary activity of the Church, *Ad Gentes*, 7 December 1965.

_____. Constitution on Sacred Liturgy, *Sacrosanctum Concilium*, 4 December 1963.

_____. Declaration on Religious Liberty, *Dignitatis Humanae*, 7 December 1965.

_____. Dogmatic Constitution on Divine Revelation, *Dei Verbum*, 18 November 1965.

_____. Dogmatic Constitution on the Church, *Lumen Gentium*, 21 November 1964.

_____. Pastoral Constitution on the Church in the modern world, *Gaudium et Spes*, 7 December 1965.

3. Authors

ALVAREZ, Tomás., *Prayer: Journeying to God with St. Teresa*, translated by A. Harriss, Boars Hill, Oxford 2019.

ANCILLI Ermanno, "Presenza di Dio," in *Dizionario Enciclopedico di Spiritualità*, Ermanno Anchilli (editor), vol. 3, Città Nuova, Rome 1995, pp. 2033-2034.

_____. "Santità Christiana," in *Dizionario Enciclopedico di Spiritualità*, Ermanno Anchilli (editor), vol. 3, Città Nuova, Rome 1995, pp. 2240-2249.

AUMANN Jordan, *Christian Spirituality in the Catholic Tradition*, Ignatius Press, Eugene OR 1985.

_____. *Spiritual Theology*, London – New York, 2006.

BIANCHI, Enzo, *Praying the Word: An Introduction to Lectio Divina*, translated by J.W. Zona, Kalamazoo, MI 1998.

BOWE, Barbara E., *Biblical Foundations of Spirituality: Touching a Finger to the Flame*, Lanham, 2017.

BURROWS, Ruth, *Ascent to Love: The Spiritual Teaching of St John of the Cross*, London 1987.

_____. *Essence of Prayer*. London: Bloomsbury Publishing, 2006.

CASTELLANO CERVERA Jesús, "La spiritualità. Ispirazione, ricerca, formazione," in *Desk. Rivista di cultura della comunicazione* 3 (Sept 1996), pp. 42-50.

_____. "Mistagogia pastorale e spiritualità" in *La spiritualità ispirazione ricerca, formazione*, Rome 1984, pp. 29-42.

_____. "Unione con Dio", in *Dizionario Enciclopedico di Spiritualità*, Ermanno Anchilli (editor), vol. 3, Città Nuova, Rome 1995, pp. 2582-2588.

CHECA Rafael, "Pastoral de espiritualidad" in *Nuevo Diccionario de Espiritualidad*, Ed. Paulinas, Madrid 1991, pp. 1484-1500.

_____. "Pastorale della Spiritualità" in *Dizionario Carmelitano*, Città Nuova, Rome 2008, pp. 654-658.

_____. *La pastoral de la espiritualidad cristiana: fundamento teológico. Sectores de actuación. Orientación mistagógica*, México 1991; Italian translation, *La pastorale della spiritualità Cristiana*, LEV, Vatican City 1998.

CUNNINGHAM Lawrence S., "Holiness", in *The New Dictionary of Catholic Spirituality*, ed. Michael Downey, TPI, Bangalore 2003, p. 481.

DREYER, Elisabeth A. *Accidental Theologians: Four Women Who Shaped Christianity*. Cincinnati, Ohio 2014.

DREYER, Elisabeth A. and BURROWS Mark S., eds., *Minding the Spirit: The Study of Christian Spirituality*, Baltimore, Maryland 2005.

DUNN James D. G., *Word Biblical Commentary: Romans 9-16*, Vol. 38B, Word Biblical Commentary, Word Incorporated, Dallas 1988

FROHLICH, Mary, ed., *Carmelite Wisdom and Prophetic Hope: Treasures Both New and Old*, Carmelite Studies 11, Washington, DC 2018.

GELLMAN, Jerome, "Mysticism and Religious Experience", in W.J. Wainwright, ed., *The Oxford Handbook of Philosophy of Religion*, Oxford 2005, 138-167.

GONZÁLEZ Luis Jorge, *Acompañamento espiritual integrador, Modelando a Jesús con la guía de su Espíritu*, Font, Monterrey Mexico 2000.

_____. *Desarrollo humano en plenitud. Teología espiritual*, Monte Carmelo, Burgos 2002; Italian translation, *Sviluppo umano in Pienezza. Teologia Spirituale*, Effata Editrice, Torino 2007.

_____. *Estimulación espiritual: tecnicas y recursos de espiritualidad pastoral*, Ediciones del Teresianum, México 2002; Italian translation, *Stimolazione Spirituale. Tecniche e risorse di spiritualità pastorale*, Edizione OCD, Rome 2004.

_____. *Misión Personal*, Teresianum, Rome 2000.

_____. *Psicología de los místicos. Desarrollo humano en plenitud*, Ediciones Del Teresianum, México 2001; Italian translation, *Psicologia dei mistici. Sviluppo umano in Pienezza*, LEV, Vatican City 2001.

GOYA Benito, *Luce e guida nel cammino. Manuale di direzione spirituale*, EDB, Bologna 2004.

HART, David Bentley, *The Experience of God: Being, Consciousness, Bliss*, New Haven 2013.

HUNT, Anne, *The Trinity: Insights from the Mystics*, Collegeville, MN 2010.

IVES Michael, *Understanding the Spiritual Exercises. Text and Commentary. A handbook for retreat Directors*, MGP, Great Britain 1998.

LAUDAZI Carlo, "Preghiera", in *Dizionario Enciclopedico di Spiritualità*, vol. 3, Città Nuova, Rome 1995, pp. 1992-2009.

_____. *L'uomo chiamato all'unione con Dio in Cristo. Temi fondamentali di teologia spirituale*, Edizioni OCD, Rome 2006.

LOHFINK, Gerhard, *Prayer Takes Us Home: The Theology and Practice of Christian Prayer*, translated by L.M. Maloney, Collegeville, MN 2020.

MARIA CECILIA DEL VOLTO SANTO, "Presenza di Dio", in *Dizionario Carmelitano*, ed. by Emanuele Boaga and Luigi Boriello, Città Nuova, Rome 2008, pp. 691-697.

MARTIN, James, *Learning to Pray: A Guide for Everyone*, Broadway, NY 2021.

MATTAM Zacharias, *Spiritual life as Christian's mystical union with Christ: not I but Christ lives in me (Galatians 2:20)*, UPS, Rome 2006.

MATTHEW, Ian, *John of the Cross, Seasons of Prayer*, Oxford 2014.

ORSATTI Mauro, "Missione," in *Dizionario Biblico della Vocazione*, ed. Giuseppe De Virgilio, Libreria Editrice Rogate, Rome 2007 pp. 565-573.

PACHO Eulogio, *Temi Fondamentali in San Giovanni della Croce*, Edizioni OCD, Rome 1989.

PERRIN David B., *Studying Christian spirituality*, Routledge, New York NY 2007.

PERRONI Marinella, "Mondo/Terra," in *Dizionario Biblico della Vocazione*, ed. Giuseppe De Virgilio, Libreria Editrice Rogate, Rome 2007, pp. 576-580.

POLLINARO Giuseppe, *Dio presente e trasformante. Saggio di teologia spirituale*, LDC, Torino 1993.

RAHNER Karl, "Conversion," in *Encyclopedia of Theology. A Concise Sacramentum Mundi*, ed. Karl Rahner, Burns & Oates, Kent GB 1993, pp. 291-295.

RUIZ SALVADOR Federico, *Caminos del Espíritu: compendio de Teología spiritual*, Editorial de esoiritualidad, Madrid, 1998; Italian translation, *Le vie dello Spirito. Sintesi di teologia spirituale*, EDB, Bologna 2004.

_____. "San Juan de la Cruz, Vida teologal durante la purificación interior," in *Revista de Espiridualidad* 18 (1959), pp. 349-356;

_____. *Introducción a san Juan de la Cruz: el escritor, los escritos, el sistema*, Biblioteca de Autores Cristianos, Madrid 1968; Italian translation, *San Giovanni della Croce, il Santo, gli scritti, il sistema*, Teresianum, Rome 1973.

_____. *Saint John of the Cross. The saint and his teaching*, Darlington Carmel, Germany 1988.

SHELDRAKE Philip, "Spirituality and Its Critical methodology", in *Exploring Christian spirituality: essays in honor of Sandra M. Schneiders*, edited by Bruce H. Lescher, and Elizabeth Liebert, Paulist Press, New York 2006, pp. 15-35.

SORRENTINO Domenico, *L'esperienza di Dio: disegno di teologia spirituale*, Cittadella, Assisi 2007.

SPINKS Bryan D. (editor), *The place of Christ in liturgical prayer: Trinity, christology, and liturgical theology*, Liturgical Press, Collegeville MN 2008.

ST. JOHN OF THE CROSS, The Collected Works of St. John of the Cross, translated by K. Kavanaugh and O. Rodriguez, Washington, DC 19912.

ST. TERESA OF JESUS, The Collected Works of St. Teresa of Jesus, 3 vol., translated by K. Kavanaugh and O. Rodriguez, Washington, DC 1976-1985; vol. 1-2: 20192.

TETLOW Joseph A., *Making choices in Christ: the foundations of Ignatian spirituality*, Loyola Press, Chicago 2008.

VON HILDEBRAND Dietrich, *Transformation in Christ: on the Christian attitude of mind*, Helicon Press, Baltimore MD 1962.

HANS URS VON BALTHASAR, "Theology and Holiness", in *Communio* 14/4 (1987), 345

INDEX

Practical Spiritual Growth Series

Volume I
LIVING THE DREAM OF GOD

Volume II
FINDING YOURSELF IN GOD, *on the identity as children of God**

Volume III
DOING THE WILL OF THE FATHER**

Volume IV
FOLLOWING AND IMITATING CHRIST**

Volume V
GUIDED BY THE HOLY SPIRIT**

Volume VI
LIVING IN THE CHURCH***

Volume VII
SERVING OTHERS WHILE CARING FOR NATURE***

** to be published in Q4 of 2022*
*** to be published before the end of Q2 of 2023*
**** to be published before the end of Q4 of 2023*

About the Author

FR DOMINIC MICHAEL SULTANA (b.1980) hails from Malta, Europe. Following his Call for the priesthood, he entered the local Diocesan Seminary and was ordained a priest in 2005.

For the past two decades, he has committed his life to research and putting into practice ways and means of spreading the Gospel effectively.

This journey led him to travel for study, ministry, and experience in different countries, including Malta, Italy, the USA, Ireland, Nigeria, and the United Kingdom.

He is a Doctor in Sacred Theology (Rome), obtained a 3-year diploma in Spiritual Counselling, and is also an Advanced Practitioner in Cognitive Coaching.

He also trained with renowned motivational speakers: Anthony Robbins, Robert J. Garmston, Claudio Belotti, Alessio Roberti, Jenny Edwards and Luis Jorge Gonzalez.

For more practical information
that can facilitate

your relationship with God
as Father, Son and Holy Spirit

and on how to live
in the Church and in society
as a child of God

visit

www.godmediation.world

Printed in Great Britain
by Amazon

18342542R00102